Favorite Bible Stories for Children

A Treasured Collection

Adapted by Tess Fries and Shawn South Aswad
Illustrated by Cheryl Mendenhall
Cover design by Shannon Osborne Thompson

DALMATIAN PRESS

ART DIRECTED BY
SHANNON OSBORNE THOMPSON

EDITED BY
CINDY ROBERTSON

ALL ART AND EDITORIAL MATERIAL IS OWNED BY DALMATIAN PRESS.
ISBN: 1-57759-420-7

FIRST PUBLISHED IN THE UNITED STATES IN 2000 BY DALMATIAN PRESS, USA

THE DALMATIAN PRESS NAME, LOGO AND SPOTTED SPINE ARE
TRADEMARKS OF DALMATIAN PRESS, FRANKLIN, TENNESSEE 37067.

11147a

00 01 02 QWK 10 9 8 7 6 5 4 3 2 1

GOD'S CREATION

Genesis 1

Long, long ago the world was very different than it is now. In fact, there was no world at all! Everything was dark and empty. But God was in the darkness, and He had a plan to make something good.

God said "Let there be light," and a golden light shone
everywhere. He called the light day and the dark night.
This was the very first day.

On the second day, God made the beautiful blue sky. He put the clouds in it to hold the raindrops, and He called the sky "Heaven."

On the third day, God made the sparkling water and formed the seas and rivers. He shaped the great mountains and the sloping valleys from the land and then sprinkled the deserts with sand. He planted the fields with tall grasses and trees and colorful flowers. And God saw that it was good.

God put lights in the sky on the fourth day. He made the brilliant sun for the daytime and the gentle light of the moon for the night. He placed each star in just the right spot and made them twinkle and shine.

On the fifth day, God made the gigantic whales and the slithering eels. He made the shark and octopus and every kind of fish to fill the waters.

9

God also made the birds to sail on the wind through the sky. He made the mighty eagles, the honking geese and the tiny hummingbirds.

The next day God made all of the animals. He made animals that hopped, roared, growled and mooed. He made some animals with antlers and some with pouches.

God wanted someone to rule over the animals, to enjoy His creation and to love Him. So on the sixth day, God also made the first man.

He made him from the dust of the ground and breathed into him the breath of life. God named him Adam.

On the seventh day, God rested, for He was finished. He saw everything He made, and He knew that it was good.

God is the maker of all things. There will never be anyone greater or more powerful than He is. God made you just the way you are. He wants you to enjoy His creation and to love Him, for He knows that this is good.

ADAM & EVE

Genesis 2

Long ago when God made the world and all that was in it, He created the very first man. The man's name was Adam. God made Adam from the dust of the ground, and then He breathed life into him.

God put Adam in a wonderful garden He had planted in Eden. There were all kinds of plants and animals and trees in the garden. Some of the trees were just beautiful to look at, while others had wonderful fruit that Adam could eat and enjoy.

In the middle of the garden God planted two very special trees.
One was the Tree of Life and the other was the Tree of
Knowledge of Good and Evil.

God told Adam, "You may eat the fruit from every tree in the garden, except from the Tree of Knowledge of Good and Evil. The day that you eat from that tree you will die."

Adam spent time in the garden tending the plants for God. It was joyful work and a happy time for Adam.

One day God brought all the marvelous creatures He had made to Adam and gave him the job of naming them.

Adam named the cattle and the frogs, the raven and the lions. Large and small, furry and scaly, Adam gave each animal its name.

After all the animals were named, God looked upon Adam and said, "It is not good for man to be alone." He caused Adam to fall into a very deep sleep.

While Adam was sleeping, God took one of the ribs
from his chest and made the first woman from it.
The woman's name was Eve. She became Adam's wife.

It was wonderful living in the garden among the
friendly animals and the beautiful plants. But the best
part was being near God, and walking and talking
with Him in the garden.

Now the serpent was more clever than any other creature in the garden. One day he came to Eve and said, "You will not die if you eat the fruit from the Tree of Knowledge of Good and Evil. God knows that if you eat it, you will become a god as He is."

Eve looked at the fruit. It was beautiful and looked like it would taste delicious. Eve decided to believe the serpent instead of God. She took the fruit and ate it. Then she gave some to Adam and he ate it, too.

At once Adam and Eve knew they had done something terribly wrong! They had disobeyed God! They were ashamed and afraid.

Later, in the cool of the day, they heard God's voice as He walked through the garden, and they hid. "Adam, where are you?" God asked. Adam said, "I heard your voice, and I was afraid." God asked Adam if he had eaten the fruit from the Tree of Knowledge of Good and Evil. Adam replied, "Eve gave me the fruit, and I ate it."

God was not happy that Adam and Eve disobeyed Him and were deceived by the serpent. He said to the serpent, "Because of this you will have to crawl on your belly from now on."

Then God told Adam and Eve, "Because you have eaten the forbidden fruit, you must leave the garden," and He drove them out of the Garden of Eden.Cherubim with flaming swords were placed at the entrance of the garden to guard it.

Adam and Eve began their new lives outside the garden. They had to make a home among the rocks and trees, and they worked hard to grow food among the thistles and weeds. But worst of all, they could no longer walk with God as they had before.

NOAH'S ARK

Genesis 6-7

Long, long ago there lived a very special man whose name was Noah. Noah was special because God chose him to do an important job.

One day God said to Noah, "I am not happy with many of the people and have decided to send a great flood to cover the earth. I want you to build a huge boat. In this boat, I want you to carry your family and two of every other living creature, so that some may be saved."

Noah began to build the large boat which was called an ark. The ark was strong and sturdy, and it was made of gopher wood. It had one window and one door. When the ark was finished, Noah gathered together plenty of food.

He needed to find enough food to feed his family and all the
animals while they lived on the ark, because they would not see
land for a long time.

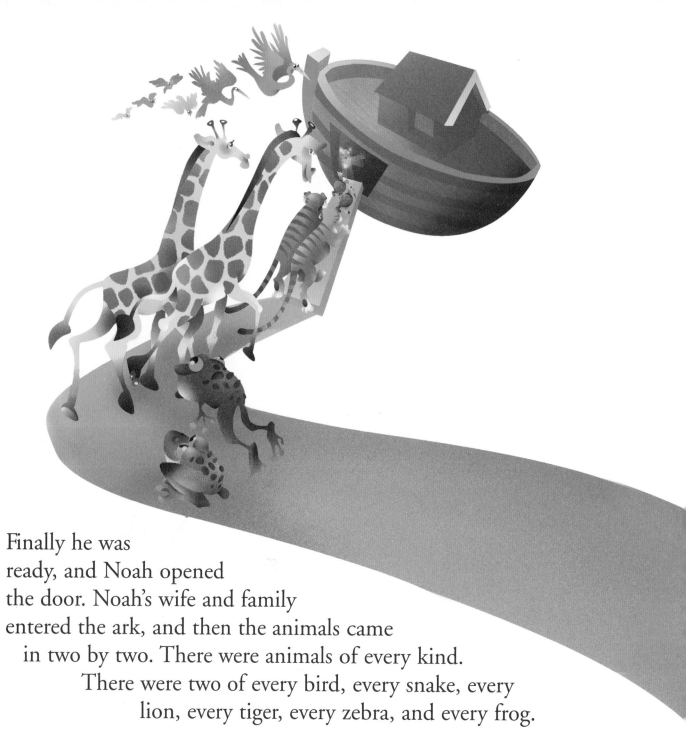

Finally he was
ready, and Noah opened
the door. Noah's wife and family
entered the ark, and then the animals came
in two by two. There were animals of every kind.
There were two of every bird, every snake, every
lion, every tiger, every zebra, and every frog.

Noah had never seen so many animals. The elephants did not look happy. "Don't worry," said Noah, "I have made the ark very large. There is plenty of room for everyone."

The birds fluttered in fear. "Don't worry," said Noah, "I have built the ark very high so you will be able to fly."

The lions roared in anger. "Don't worry," said Noah, "I have gathered lots of food. There will be plenty for everyone to eat."

After every animal was safely on the ark, they heard a loud rumble.
It was the sound of thunder…and then the rain began to fall.

The rain poured down for forty days and forty nights. Water covered the earth, and Noah's ark rose high on the water.

One day the ark hit something and came to a stop. It made a terrible ruckus. The giraffes fell on the zebras, the zebras fell on the lions, and the lions fell on the frogs. When everyone stood up again, they found themselves resting on top of a high mountain.

Noah sent a dove away from the ark to see if the land was dry. When the dove came back, Noah knew the earth was still under water. Noah sent out the dove a second time, and this time it brought back an olive leaf. This was a sign that the flood was over.

"Hooray!" cried Noah. "The earth is dry again. We can all get off the ark!" The animals were excited and could hardly wait for Noah to open the door. When the door was opened, the animals rushed outside. The birds flew high in the sky while the snakes slithered low in the fresh grass.

Noah said good-bye to the animals as they paraded off to find new homes. The elephants lumbered over the new land looking for food. The giraffes glided past in search of tall trees. The frogs hopped playfully towards the ponds. And every other living thing discovered a new place to live.

"Noah," said God, "I am very pleased with your work, and I promise never to destroy the earth with water again. Look to the sky between the clouds for a sign of my promise and love." Noah looked up, and in the sky was the most beautiful thing he had ever seen. It was a rainbow full of bright colors.

JOSEPH
& His Coat of Many Colors
Genesis 37

Once there was an old man named Jacob who had twelve sons. Of all his sons he loved Joseph the most, and he gave him a beautiful coat of bright colors.

Joseph's brothers were very jealous for they knew Joseph was their father's favorite son.

Joseph had two strange dreams about golden sheaves of corn and sparkling stars bowing before him. The dreams meant that one day he would be greater than his brothers. His brothers were so angry! They couldn't believe that Joseph thought they would ever bow before him.

One day Jacob asked Joseph to go to his brothers who were many miles away taking care of their sheep and cattle. He wanted to know if all was well.

When Joseph's brothers saw him coming they became so angry they wanted to get rid of him.

Reuben, the oldest brother, told them to throw Joseph into a pit. He didn't really want to hurt Joseph and planned to rescue him later. So they tore off his colorful coat and threw him deep into the pit. Joseph begged his brothers to let him out. He was so afraid!

A short time later when Reuben was gone, some traveling merchants came by, and the brothers got another idea. They pulled Joseph from the pit and sold him to the merchants for twenty pieces of silver.

When they got home, they showed their father Joseph's coat and told him that wild animals had killed Joseph. Jacob cried because he thought Joseph was dead.

The merchants took Joseph to Egypt. He looked at the towering pyramids and the great Nile River and wondered what would happen to him. Maybe he thought that God had forgotten about him. But God was with Joseph.

Joseph was sold to a rich man named Potiphar. Potiphar liked Joseph because he was a hard worker. Joseph was cheerful and always told the truth.

One day Joseph was suddenly thrown into a prison. Potiphar thought Joseph had done something terrible, but he was innocent.

Joseph probably felt all alone in prison, but God was with him.

The butler and the baker for the king of Egypt were in prison with Joseph. One night they each had a scary dream. God helped Joseph tell them what their dreams meant.

Soon the butler went back to work for the King. Two long years later when the King had a strange dream the butler remembered Joseph. He thought Joseph could help the King understand his dream, so the King sent for Joseph.

Again, God helped Joseph and he told the King about his dreams. Joseph said, "God is showing you what He is going to do." He explained to the King that for seven years there will be plenty of food for everyone. After that there will be seven years with so little food that many people will starve. Joseph also told the King how to save food now so there would be enough for everyone later.

The King knew God had made Joseph wise, so he made Joseph ruler over all of Egypt. When Joseph rode through the streets, all the people bowed before him.

Joseph forgave his brothers and invited his family to come live with him.

MOSES
Baby in the Bulrushes
Exodus 2

My name is Miriam. I am an Israelite who lived long ago in Egypt with my family. The ruler of Egypt was called "Pharaoh." He made slaves of all Israelites.

We had to work very hard and quickly in the blazing sun. Some of us made bricks for the grand buildings in Egypt. Others planted and harvested Pharaoh's crops.

One day my mother had a baby. We were so happy! We loved my baby brother very much. My mother had to hide my brother from Pharaoh's soldiers. She told me that Pharaoh had commanded, "Every son that is born will be thrown into the river, and every daughter will be saved." Pharaoh was afraid the baby boys would grow up to be strong men who would fight against him.

As my brother grew, it became harder to hide him. One day Mother made a sturdy basket from some bulrush leaves. She rubbed the outside of the basket with tar and mud so it would float on water.

Mother put the baby in the basket and took him to the river. She was going to hide him among the reeds at the bank of the river. The basket floated like a little boat, gently rocking in and around the plants near the water's edge.

I hid in the distance and watched to make sure my brother was safe. Suddenly, I heard people coming! I peeked out from my hiding spot and saw Pharaoh's beautiful daughter walking with her maids along the river. I held my breath and tried not to move. Then the princess saw the little boat of leaves!

One of the maids picked up the basket and carried it to the princess. What would she do when she saw my brother? As Pharaoh's daughter opened the basket, my brother began to cry. The princess knew he was an Israelite. But I could tell by the gentle look on her face that she felt sorry for him.

I stepped out from the reeds and asked the princess,
"Would you like me to call a nurse to care for the child
for you?" She told me to go find one, and I ran to get my
mother. We brought my little brother home and took
care of him for many happy months!

When he was still a little boy, my brother
had to go to the palace to live with the
princess. She named him Moses,
and he became her son.

Moses grew strong
and tall and lived like a
royal prince in the palace.
But he always knew he was
an Israelite and was sad his
people were slaves.

One day when Moses was a young man, he went out to the fields. There he saw an Egyptian soldier cruelly hitting a slave. Moses saw that no one was watching, so he went to the slave and killed the soldier. He hid the soldier in the sand and told no one what had happened.

When Moses went out the next day, he saw two Israelites fighting one another. He asked, "Why are you hurting your brother?" The Israelites were angry with Moses and said, "Who made you a prince and a judge over us? Are you going to kill us like you killed the Egyptian?" Then Moses was afraid that everyone knew he had killed the soldier.

When Pharaoh found out what Moses had done, he was very angry! Moses ran away into the desert.

MOSES
Parting the Red Sea
Exodus 3-14

Moses fled to the land of Midian. In Midian, Moses married a shepherdess and took care of her father's sheep.

One day while Moses was watching the sheep, he saw a bush covered in flames, but it didn't burn up! God spoke to Moses from within the bush, "Moses!" And Moses said, "Here I am." "Do not come any closer," God said. "Take off your shoes. You are standing on holy ground." Moses took off his shoes and hid his face because he was afraid.

Then God said, "I have seen how my people are suffering in their slavery and have come to rescue them. I am sending you to Pharaoh to tell him to let my people go." Moses was afraid and said, "Lord, they will not believe me and I will not know what to say or how to say it!"

But God told Moses, "Take your brother Aaron with you to speak
to the people. I will be with you both." So Moses took his wife
and sons and started back to Egypt.

Moses and Aaron stood before Pharaoh and said, "Let God's people go so they can worship Him or He will send plagues on Egypt." Pharaoh said, "I don't know your God. And I will not let your people go."

So God turned all of the water into blood. The fish died and there was no water to drink. Even the pitchers and pots in the homes held blood instead of water. But the Pharaoh would not let the people go.

Then God sent thousands and thousands of frogs. They filled the river and came into the houses. Frogs were on beds and in ovens and on tables. Frogs were everywhere! Pharaoh said to Moses, "Ask your God to take all of the frogs away, and then I will let your people go." But when the frogs were gone, Pharaoh still said, "No!"

God told Moses, "Have Aaron strike the ground with his rod."
So he did and instantly the sand became millions of lice! The
lice crawled over every animal, man, woman and child. It was
terrible! Then Moses said to Pharaoh, "Let my people go."
And Pharaoh said, "No!"

So God sent swarms of flies into Pharaoh's house and the houses of his servants. Soon flies covered the entire land. Pharaoh told Moses, "I will let everyone go, just ask your God to take these flies away!" But when the flies were gone, Pharaoh changed his mind and would not let the people go.

God sent sickness and sores, hail and locusts. Each time Pharaoh begged Moses to ask God to take the new trouble away.

Each time Moses did, but still Pharaoh would not let the people go.

Then God told Moses to
stretch his hand toward the sky and
a thick darkness covered Egypt for three
days. Again Pharaoh sent for Moses, "Go, but
your animals must stay in Egypt." Moses said, "Our
animals must go with us to serve the Lord." So Pharaoh
would not let the people go. God told Moses, "I will bring one
more plague. After this, Pharaoh will let you go."

At midnight, God caused all of the firstborn to die. Death
passed over only those homes with the blood of a lamb on the
doorway. Pharaoh's own son died. In his great sorrow, Pharaoh
called for Moses and said, "Leave Egypt. Take your people and
animals and go."

For 430 years the Israelites had been slaves in Egypt. Now they packed all that they had and left and followed Moses out of Egypt. God led them in a pillar of cloud at day and a pillar of fire at night. Soon, they came to the edge of the Red Sea.

When Pharaoh heard that the Israelites had fled, he changed his mind and said, "What have I done?" So the Pharaoh and his army chased the Israelites. When the Israelites saw the Egyptians, they were afraid! Then God told Moses, "Lift up your rod over the water."

Everyone watched as Moses lifted up his rod and God rolled the sea back so the people could walk through on dry ground.

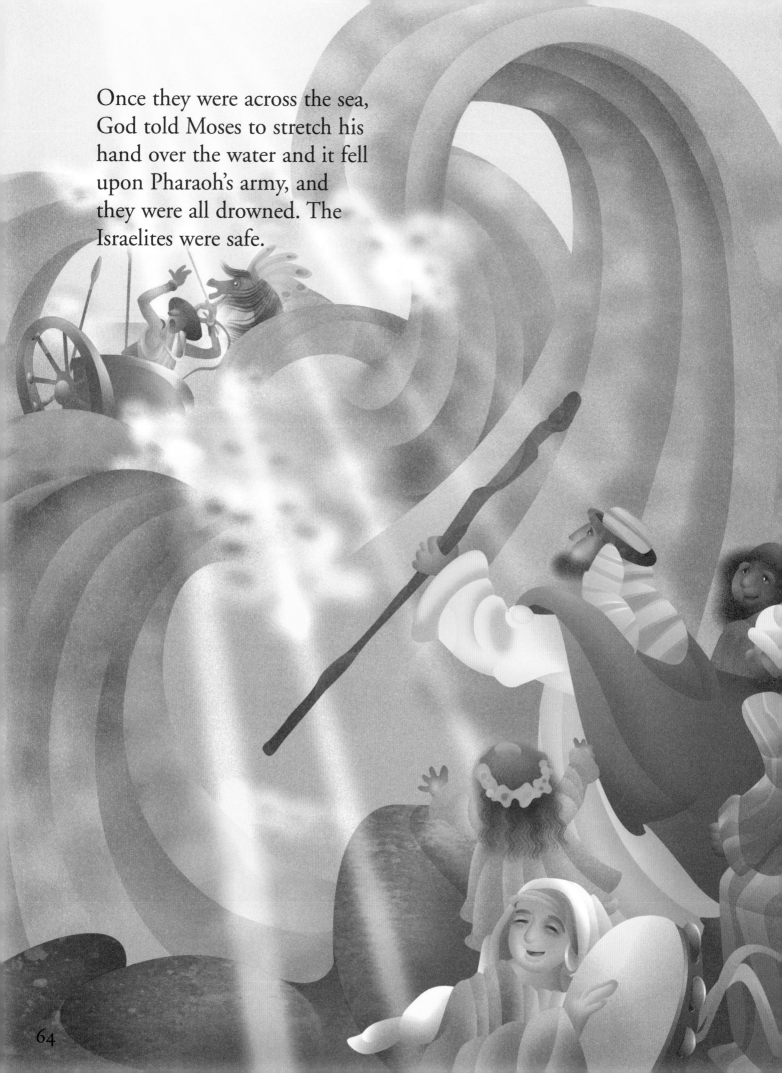

Once they were across the sea,
God told Moses to stretch his
hand over the water and it fell
upon Pharaoh's army, and
they were all drowned. The
Israelites were safe.

SAMSON & DELILAH

Judges 13; 16

Long ago God chose a man named Samson to win a great victory over his enemies, the Philistines. He was very strong, so strong that he once killed a lion with his bare hands! God had told Samson never to cut his hair. He would always be strong as long as he obeyed God. But Samson did not always do the things God wanted him to do and this brought trouble to many people.

Samson fell in love with a woman named Delilah. So the Philistines asked her to find the secret of Samson's strength. Many times she asked him, "Tell me the secret of your strength."

At first he told her, "If I was tied with seven new bowstrings I would be as weak as any man." So she tied Samson with new bowstrings and cried, "The Philistines are upon us!" In an instant Samson snapped the strings as if they were just threads.

Delilah asked again what made him so strong. He told her to tie him with new ropes and then to weave his long hair into fabric on a loom. Each time she called, "Samson, the Philistines are upon us." But each time he easily broke free.

Delilah continued to ask what caused his great might. Finally he told her, "If my head is shaved, then my strength will be gone."

When Samson fell asleep, Delilah told his enemies to cut his hair. When Samson woke up, his strength was gone! The Philistines blinded him and put him in prison. Bronze shackles were put around his ankles, and he was put to work turning the heavy wheel to grind their wheat. As time passed, Samson's hair began to grow back.

One day when the Philistines were having a big celebration in their temple. They shouted, "Bring out Samson to entertain us!" Samson prayed, "Oh God, give me strength just one more time." Then he put his hands on the two pillars beside him and pushed with all his might, and the walls of the temple crashed down on top of all the people in it.

NAOMI & RUTH

Ruth 1-4

Naomi, her husband and two sons moved to the land of Moab because there was a famine in their land of Bethlehem in Judah. After they had lived there for ten years, her husband and two sons died. So, Naomi was left alone.

She decided to travel back to Bethlehem. She said to her sons' wives, "Go, return to your mother's house and may the Lord be as kind to you as you have been to me."

One of the wives kissed Naomi good-bye and left her. But Ruth begged Naomi, "Do not make me leave you. Where you go, I will go. Where you live, I will live. Your people will be my people, and your God will be my God." Naomi saw how much Ruth loved her and wanted to be with her so together they walked the many miles back to Naomi's home.

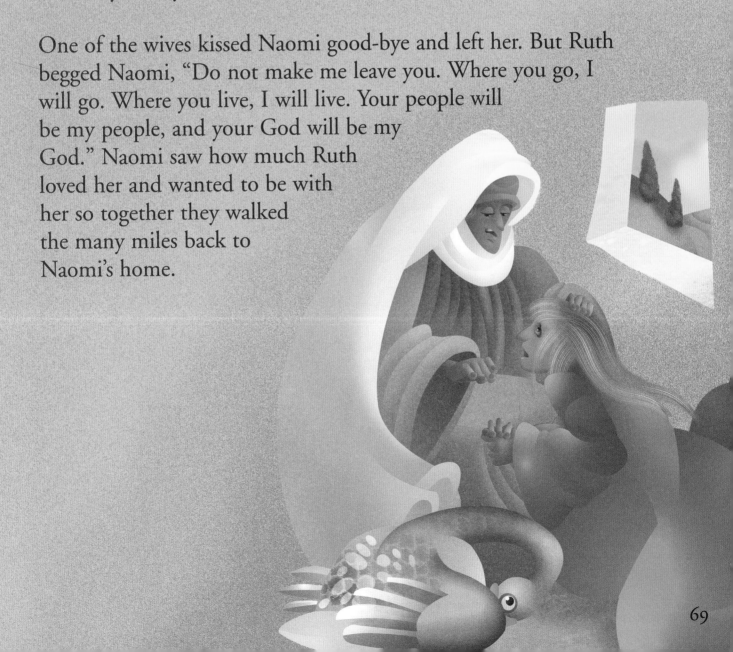

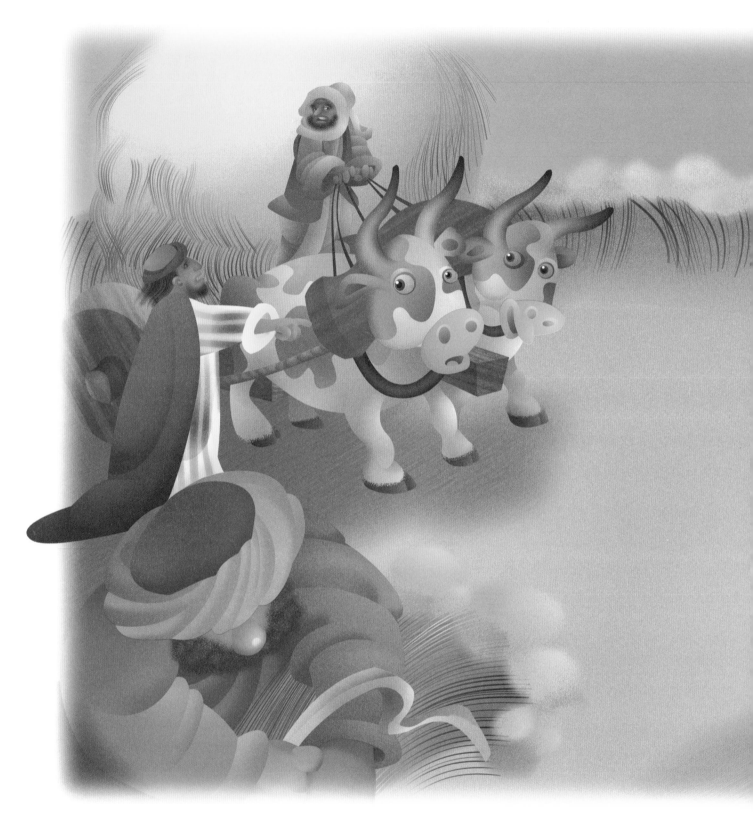

Finally, they came to Bethlehem and it was harvest time. They had no one to take care of them. People were working hard in the fields cutting the ripe barley. There was always some barley left behind in the fields for the poor to gather to eat. When Ruth heard about this she said to Naomi, "Let me go now and pick up the grain that is left behind."

Ruth began to work in the fields owned by a rich man named Boaz. When he came to the field he saw Ruth and asked, "Who is this young woman?" His servant said she was from Moab taking care of her mother-in-law, Naomi. Boaz grew to love Ruth who was very patient and worked hard. He told his servants to be sure to leave extra barley for her to gather.

When the harvest was over there was a great feast. When Boaz saw Ruth he said, "May the Lord bless you, young woman. All the city knows that you are a good woman." Boaz married Ruth and took her to live in his beautiful home. They were very happy. Ruth loved Naomi and was kind to her mother-in-law. And God took care of Ruth.

DAVID &
GOLIATH

I Samuel 17

There was a young shepherd boy named David who loved God very much. He wrote and sang many songs that told about God's power and His love for us.

One day, David's father asked him to take food to his three older brothers who were fighting in the army for King Saul. As David ran to his brothers, he saw a giant of a man named Goliath at the enemy's camp. Goliath was the biggest man David had ever seen!

Every morning and every night for forty days Goliath shouted to King Saul's soldiers saying, "If any of you can defeat me, your King's army will be the winner of the whole battle."

The King's soldiers were so afraid that they ran away when they saw Goliath. But David was not afraid. He went to the King and told him that he would fight Goliath. King Saul said, "You are too young to fight this great giant."

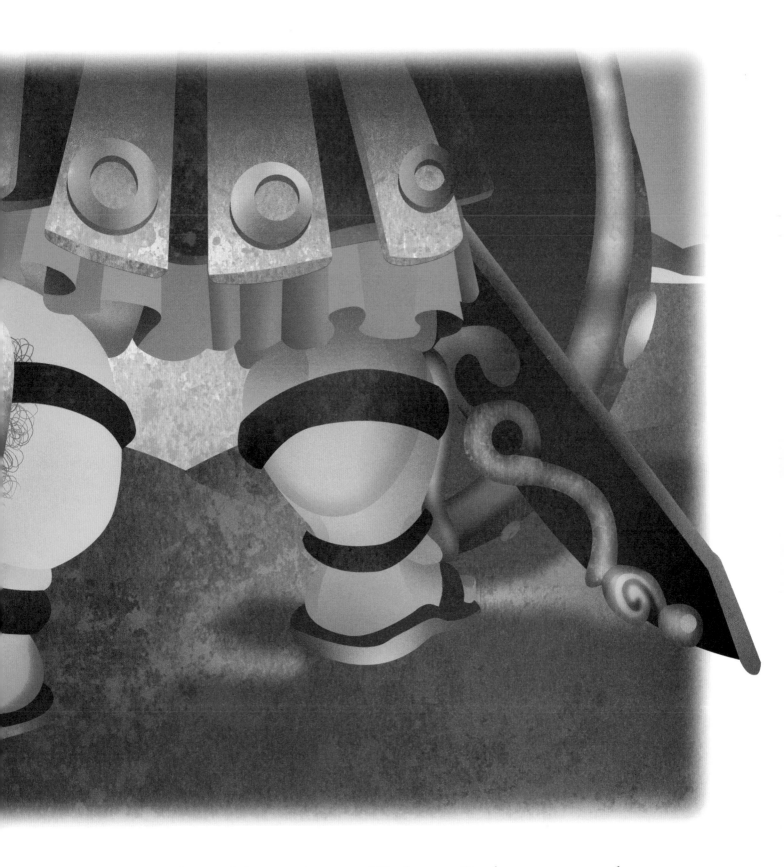

But David would not give up. He knew God was greater than any man. He told the King how, with God's help, he had defeated a lion and a bear who stole a lamb from his flock. David was sure that God would help him fight Goliath!

King Saul said to David, "You must take my armor and sword to fight a giant." David tried on the armor and the sword, but he was not used to such heavy things, so he took only his staff and sling and five smooth stones.

Then David walked toward Goliath. Goliath laughed when he saw the small boy coming down the mountain toward him.

David said, "I am not afraid! God will help me win." Then he reached into his bag and pulled out one stone.

David put the stone in his sling and hurled it toward Goliath. It hit the giant directly on the forehead, and he fell to the ground with a thud.

When the enemy soldiers saw that their mighty giant had fallen, they all ran away in fear. David had won the battle for King Saul because God had helped him!

Daniel
& The Lions' Den
Daniel 6

Daniel had been taught at home about God, and he prayed to God every morning, noon, and night. He knew God was helping him to do his work well. Because Daniel was honest and wise, the King put him in charge of his kingdom and Daniel never made any mistakes.

Other men working for the king were jealous of Daniel. They didn't want him to rule over them, so they tried to catch him doing something wrong. But Daniel only did what was right. Because he knew that his wisdom came from God, he prayed faithfully three times every day.

The bad men knew they would have to trap Daniel into doing something wrong if they wanted to get rid of him. So they went to the king and said "Oh King, make it a law that for 30 days no one can ask anyone but you for help. Anyone who breaks the law will be thrown into the lions' den."

The king thought this was a wonderful idea. He didn't know the men were trying to trap Daniel.

Daniel heard about the new law, but he still went to his room to pray and to ask God to help him do what was right.

When the sneaky men saw Daniel praying, they ran to the king and said, "Daniel has been praying to his God instead of asking you for help. He must be thrown into the lions' den!"

How sad the king was! He didn't want to hurt Daniel. He tried for
a long time to think of a way to save Daniel, but he couldn't
change the law.

Finally, the king ordered Daniel to be thrown into the den with the hungry, roaring lions. He called to Daniel, "Your God, whom you serve, will save you!"

The next morning the king ran to the den and shouted, "Daniel, has your God saved you?" Daniel answered, "God sent an angel to close the lions' mouths." The king was so happy that he made a new law that his kingdom should always pray to the God that saved Daniel from the lions.

JONAH
& The Big Fish
Jonah 1-2

God decided to send a man named Jonah to warn the people of Nineveh to change their terrible ways or He would destroy the city. But Jonah didn't obey. He ran to the sea and got on a ship that was sailing far away for Nineveh. He thought he could run away from God.

But God knew where Jonah was and He sent a fierce storm that caused the sea to be rough and rolling. The sailors were afraid. They called on their gods to quiet the storm but the winds blew harder and the waves grew higher.

They thought the boat would sink so they threw some of the ship's load overboard. But it didn't help.

All of this time Jonah had been sleeping in the bottom of the ship. The captain woke him up and said "What are you doing? Get up and ask your God to save us or we will drown!"

Jonah said to the terrified sailors "Throw me overboard and the sea will be calm again. I know this storm has come because of me." The sailors didn't want to throw Jonah into the sea. They rowed and rowed trying to get the ship safely to shore, but the storm only got worse.

Finally, the sailors knew they must do as Jonah said. They picked Jonah up and threw him into the furious sea. The wind stopped blowing, the sea became calm and the ship sailed away.

Jonah went deeper and deeper into the sea, but he didn't drown.
God sent a huge fish to swallow Jonah whole and he stayed in the
belly of the fish for three days and nights.

Jonah was very frightened. He prayed to God from inside the fish.
He was sorry he had disobeyed.

God listened to Jonah's prayers and He caused the fish to spit up Jonah onto a sandy beach. Then God told Jonah to go to the people of Nineveh and warn them to be good.

They heard Jonah's warnings and were afraid. So they all wore sackcloth and prayed for forgiveness.

God did not punish the people of Nineveh because He loved them, and He knew that they were truly sorry.

THE BIRTH OF A SAVIOR

Luke 1-2

God sent the angel Gabriel to Mary, who was a virgin. She was soon to marry a man named Joseph. The angel said, "Don't be afraid, Mary, for you have found favor with God. You will have a son and you will name him Jesus." "How will this be?" asked Mary. Gabriel answered, "The Holy Spirit will come upon you. The child will be the Son of God. Nothing is impossible with God."

The Roman ruler had commanded everyone to go to the town where their families were from so they could be counted. So Mary and Joseph traveled to his family's town of Bethlehem, the city of David. They had to travel even though Mary was going to have a baby very soon.

At last they arrived in Bethlehem. Joseph went from inn to inn, looking for one that had a room where he and Mary could rest, but every inn was full. Finally Joseph led Mary to a stable where she could lie down.

The time came for the baby to be born, and she gave birth to her firstborn, a son. She wrapped him in cloths and placed him in a manger where the animals ate and slept.

Not far from the stable were shepherds in a field watching their sheep during the night when suddenly the angel of the Lord came to them. The shepherds were so afraid! But the angel said, "Fear not, for I bring you tidings of great joy which shall be to all people. For unto you is born this day in the city of David a Savior, which is Christ the Lord.

And you shall find the baby wrapped in swaddling clothes and lying in a manger."

All at once there were many angels singing, praising God and saying, "Glory to God in the highest, and on earth, peace, good will toward men."

Then the beautiful singing was over and the angels went back
to heaven. The shepherds left their flocks of sheep and ran
quickly to the city. There, in the humble stable, they found
Mary and Joseph. The baby Jesus, the infant Savior, was lying
on the straw in the manger.

How excited they were! They left the stable full of joy and repeated to everyone they met the words the angel had spoken to them.

As they walked back to the fields they praised God for showing them the long awaited Savior.

The Son of God had come as a little babe, born in a simple stable, someday to save all of mankind by his death on the cross. How great and wonderful is God's love for us!